studies in bach for

saxophone and treble clef instruments

BACH SHAPES II

Jon De Lucia

MUSÆUM CLAUSUM PRESS
2021

Dedicated to two of
the biggest teachers in my life
that we lost in 2020,
Richard Kenneally and Lee Konitz.

Copyright © 2021 by Musæum Clausum Press

All rights reserved. This book or any portion thereof may not be reproduced or used in any manner whatsoever without the express written permission of the publisher except for the use of brief quotations in a book review.

Musæum Clausum Press
311 6th St. #2
Brooklyn, NY 11215

ISBN : 9781737281948

Ingram Edition: Musaeum Clausum

Visit bachshapes.com/resources to get access to the Bach Shapes Resource Library, which includes accompaniment audio tracks, tutorial videos, free PDFs and more.

Book Design & Production: Chrissy Kurpeski

Music Composition & Layout: Jon De Lucia

TABLE OF CONTENTS

Introduction.. v

The Grand Scale Exercise x

BOOK ONE

Diatonic Shapes by Key 2

    Sources of Diatonic Shapes........................... 3

    Shapes in C Major 7

    Shapes in F Major 12

    Shapes in Bb Major 16

    Shapes in Eb Major 20

    Shapes in Ab Major 24

    Shapes in Db Major 28

    Shapes in F# Major 32

    Shapes in B Major 36

    Shapes in E Major 40

    Shapes in A Major 44

    Shapes in D Major 48

    Shapes in G Major 52

Minor and Diminished Shapes 56

    Jazz Etude "Diminished Delight" 67

End of Book One

BOOK TWO

Circle of Fifths Harmonic Sequences.................. 76
   Jazz Etude "Feel The Kern".......................... 89
   Jazz Etude "Kosmapolitano".......................... 90

Circle of Fifths Progression with Dominant Chords.... 92
   Jazz Etude "Exploration in Fifths".................. 94

Bach and Paul Desmond 96
   Jazz Etude "A Tadd Baroque"......................... 100
   Jazz Solo "Wintersong" 101

Bach Loops 104

Arpeggiation 114
   Jazz Etude "Cheroque" 117

Additional Etudes................................. 124
   Jazz Etude "Going Bach Home"....................... 125
   Jazz Etude "Musaeum Clausum"....................... 126
   Jazz Etude "Jesu, Jes' Me" 127
   Jazz Etude "Love Me or Liebe Me"................... 128

INTRODUCTION

I am very excited to present a second volume of exercises straight out of the music of Johann Sebastian Bach. I didn't know if I'd be writing a second book; and now I don't know if I'll write a third, as I have included so much more content in this volume than I had intended originally. I see the book before you as a great compendium of *ideas* that a musician of any background can put to use in myriad ways. Book One is a continuation of the first *Bach Shapes:* more diatonic sequences. Some changes include: more up and down sequences, which sometimes meant combining two different shapes; different articulations in each key; modes other than major; keys arranged in the circle of fifths as opposed to the "Rubank" order. My goal here is less purist, more practical and fun. Thus you'll notice a few patterns included from outside of the world of Bach. Added to this section is a new chapter on minor and diminished patterns, including some jazz oriented studies.

In Book Two, you'll find even more to apply as a jazz musician, but also some instrument focused studies to really dig in on your technique on any instrument. First, the all important circle of fifths progression is fully explored in its diatonic and dominant forms. This leads into a short consolidation of a few articles I have published on the great saxophonist Paul Desmond's use of these types of shapes in a jazz setting, great for learning how to apply the shapes to changes. After that I introduce a new concept with "Bach Loops." Akin to the looping exercises woodwind players might recognize from Baermann, Kroepsch, Klosé or others, these are finger and chop busters designed to iron out your technique but also work on your musical phrasing. Really fun to play. I then discuss Bach's use of arpeggiation, and how that can be a great way to work through a standard tune, including exercises and etudes. Closing out the book are a few more jazz oriented etudes utilizing Bach's melodic material. As a bonus, if you are playing an Eb instrument, you will find live backing tracks for most of the etudes in the book on bachshapes.com/resources. If you would like other transpositions of the etudes, check out my *Bach Shapes: The Etudes* books, which compile most of the etudes here and the four from *Bach Shapes I*. On the site above I have also provided MIDI accompaniment for the circle of fifths sequences at the beginning of Book Two.

How To Practice

As with the first Bach Shapes, this book may be practiced a variety of ways. While most of the exercises have been transposed into every key for you, it is a key skill to be able to transpose these shapes on your own; the given examples are there to show you how. New to this book are a number of stand-alone exercises that cycle through all twelve keys, along with some more open ended jazz studies. Get creative and share some of the ways you practice with me! I've learned a lot from how people were using the first book and have implemented some new ideas here. There is a ton of material to get down and I hope it is useful to you. I include these words from the first book:

> ". . . the improviser can then utilize these melodic shapes in their own spontaneous lines. The key word is spontaneous. Though these exercises have value when practiced methodically at home, the key is then to forget them and allow them to naturally occur in your improvising. Nothing is more deadly to real improvisation than mechanically running patterns through tunes on the bandstand. As the great Jimmy Giuffre said, 'The music is you, and must always breathe fire. Never let it run straight and dry.' Happy Practicing!"

—Jon De Lucia, February 2021

There are as many non-saxophonists using these books as there are saxophonists now, but I am including some sax-specific embouchure notes below from the first book.

Embouchure Notes

It is crucial to have a relaxed but firm embouchure to play these exercises. The lower lip will roll out to accommodate the higher pitches, roll back for the lower, but as Joe Allard says, do not drop the jaw. Strive for an "inclusive" embouchure that is relaxed enough to drop down large intervals but firm enough to reach high F. Practice the exercises slowly and check for evenness of sound and proper intonation, especially when approaching the altissimo notes.

A PRACTICAL EXAMPLE

Let's take a look at Shape #9 from *Bach Shapes I* in C Major.

It would be beneficial to isolate the first measure only, like this:

The widest interval here is the octave, C2 – C3.

Start by playing this interval, checking tuning and resonance. By resonance I mean that you should be achieving the full tonal color of each note, including a wide spectrum of overtones. If familiar with overtone practice, check the C's against your low C overtone fingering and work to center your sound before proceeding. More information on how to practice overtones can be found in Sigurd Rascher's *Top Tones for the Saxophone* and Dave Liebman's *Developing a Personal Saxophone Sound*. You will discover that you may have to take in more reed as you go up the octave. This is preferable to squeezing to ascend, or dropping the jaw to descend. A slight moving forward of lower lip along with a steady balance of firmness should achieve the intended sound.

Once your octave is established, maintain that feeling as you begin the exercise. The C's are your goalposts, to remain steady as you fill in the intervals between them. It may be beneficial to further break down the measure into 4-note groupings. Like this:

Other combinations are certainly possible. Practice all of the exercises slowly, considering these concepts until comfortable.

In terms of fingering difficulties, isolate any one particularly difficult interval and practice it at a steady tempo in the following rhythms, staying in any one measure until comfortable:

By breaking things down in this manner, one can find much to improve on in these exercises.

The Grand Scale Exercise
Adapted From Brandenburg Concerto V

Try a variety of articulations. Harmonic analysis is included for the first pass, the same progression continues through all 12 keys.

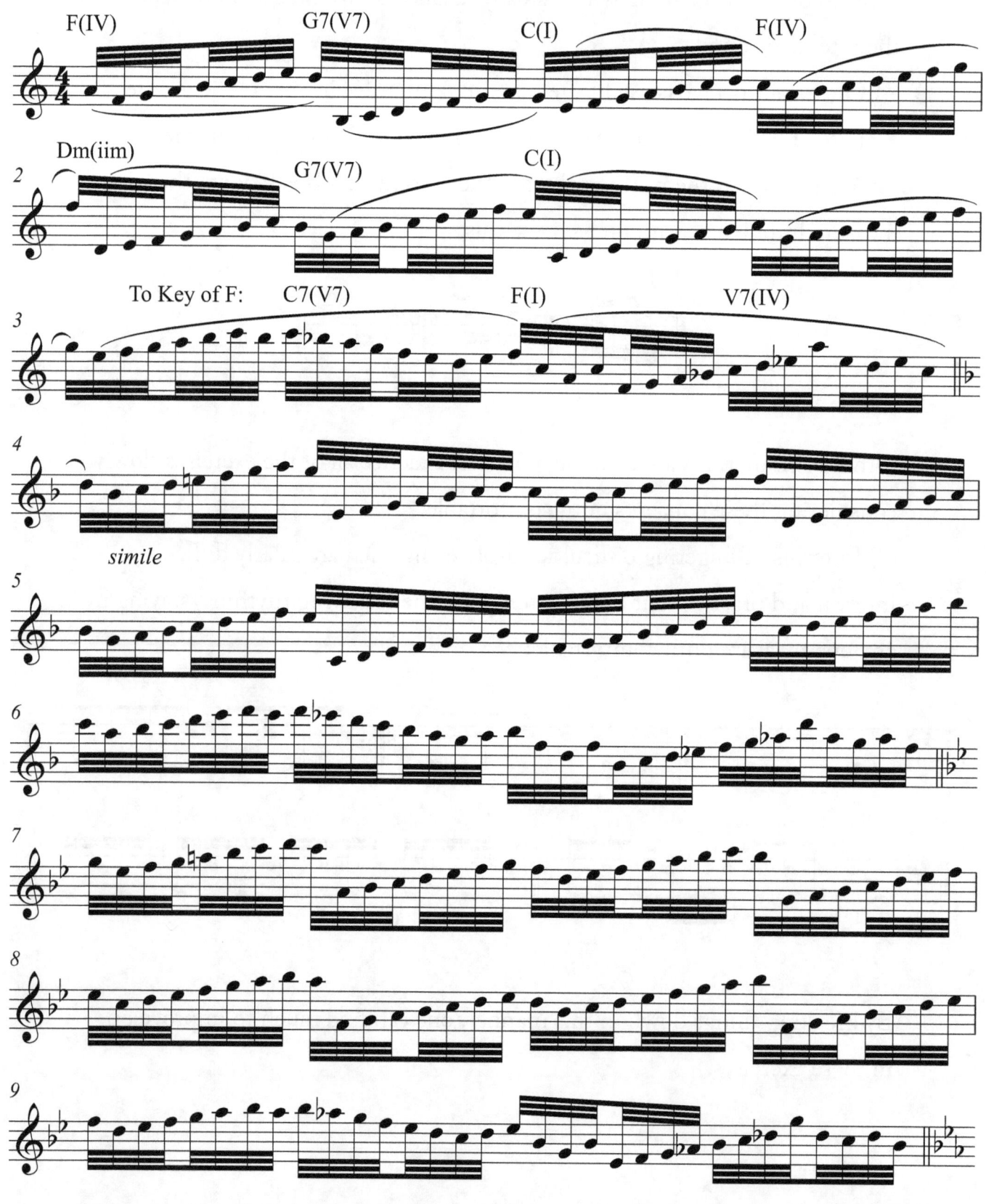

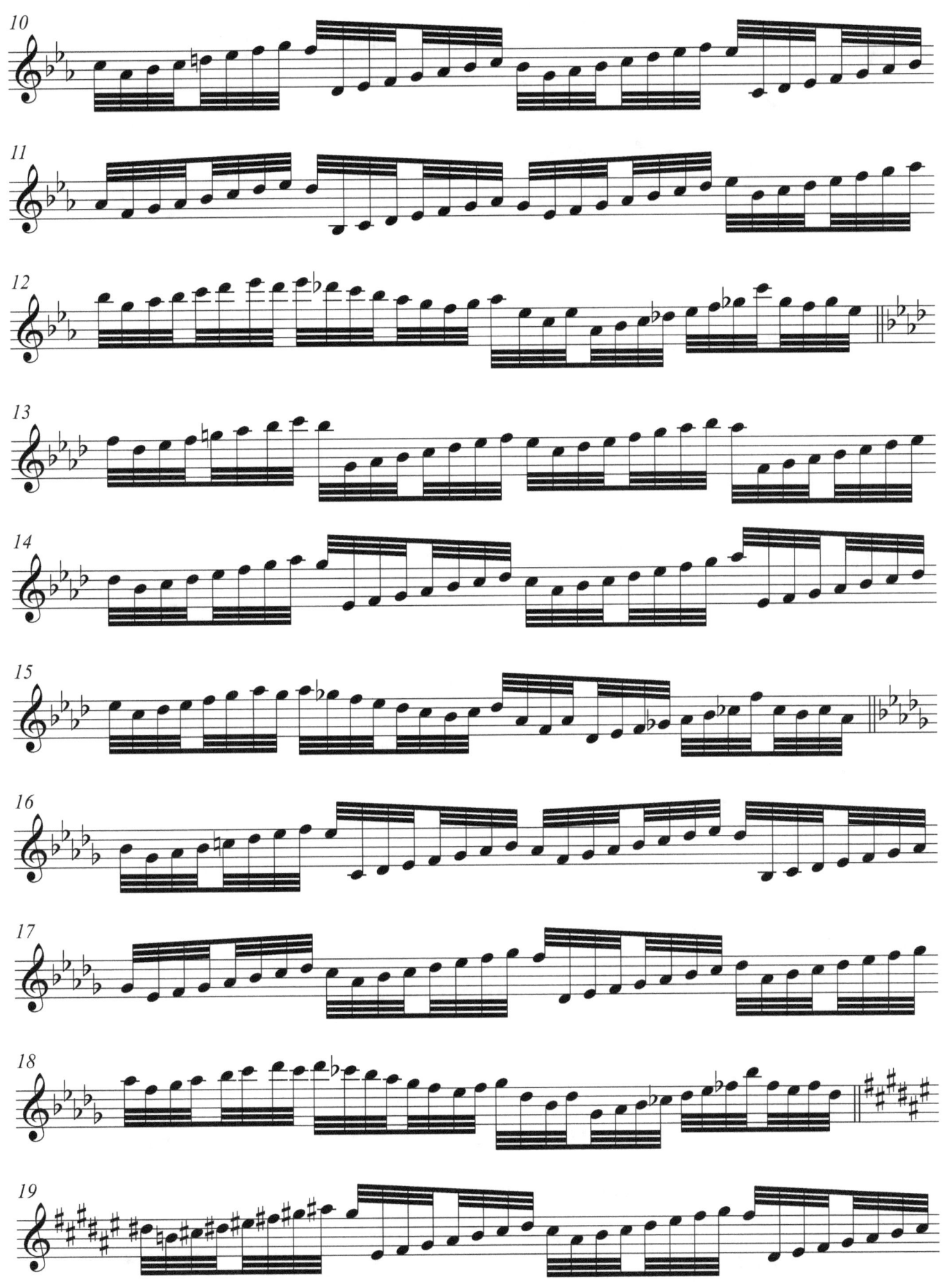

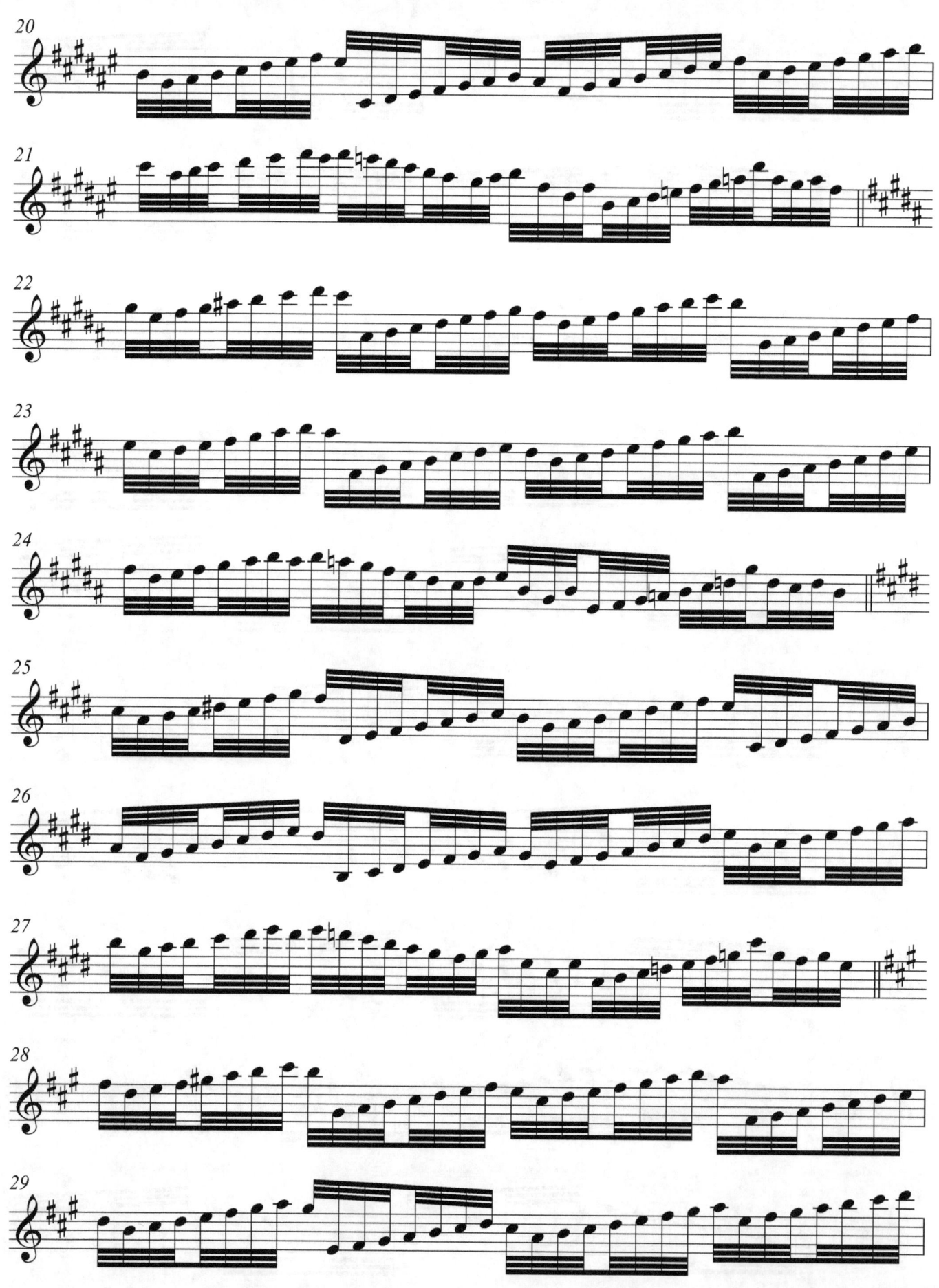

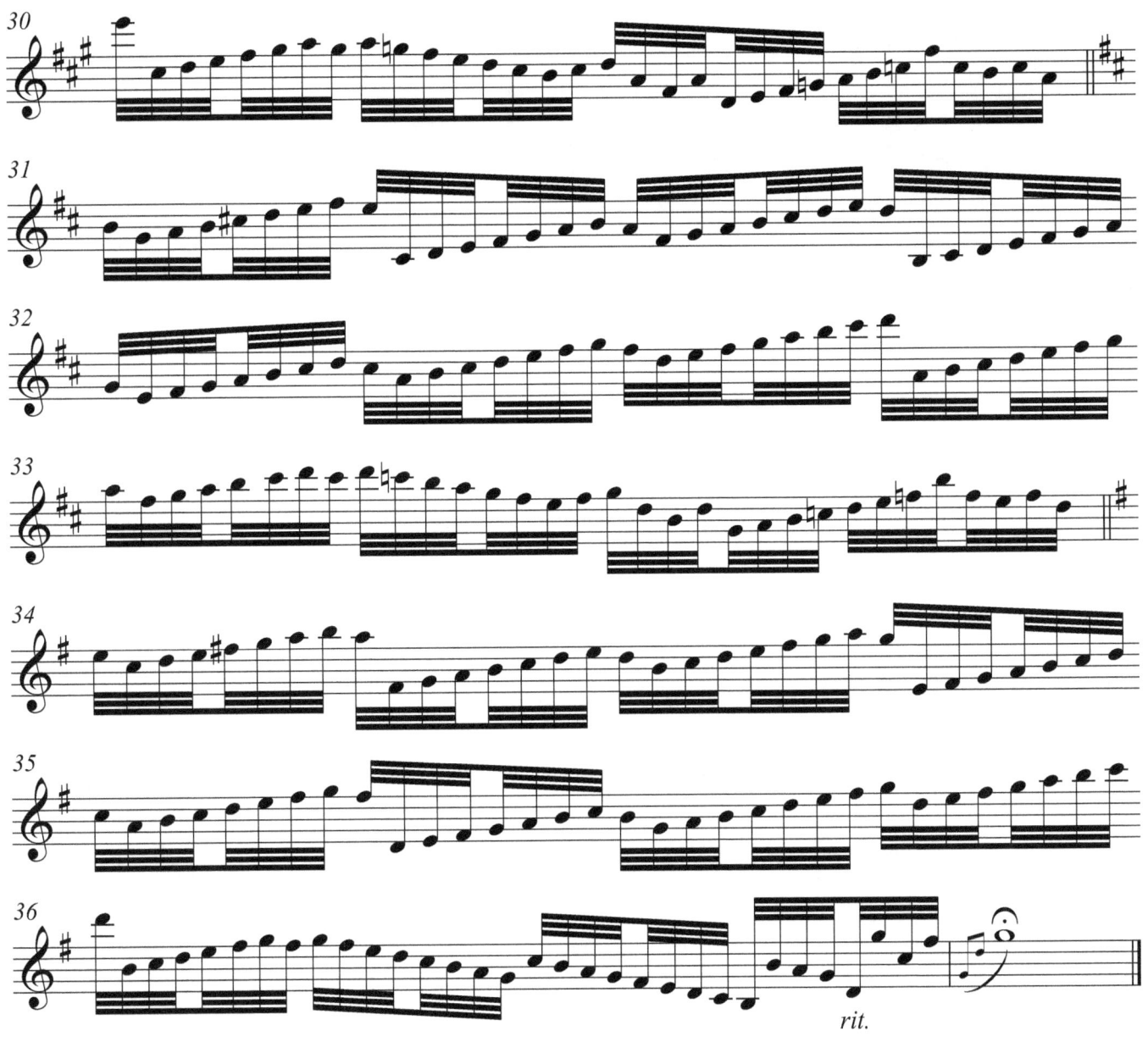

If they think they are doing something new,
they ought to do what I do every day—
spend at least two hours every day
listening to **JOHANN SEBASTIAN BACH**
and, man, it's all there.

If they want to improvise around a theme,
which is the essence of jazz,
they should learn from the master.
He never wastes a note, and he knows where
every note is going and when to bring it back.

Some of these cats go way out and forget
where they began or what they started to do.
BACH will clear it up for them.

—COLEMAN HAWKINS

BOOK ONE

DIATONIC SHAPES BY KEY

In this section you will find a variety of diatonic shapes from Bach's music and a couple of my own invention. New to this book is the addition of articulations, which vary from key to key to give you a wealth of options. Of course you may choose to apply your own articulations. Similarly, rather than present things the same way in every key, I have presented some of the exercises in different modes: Harmonic Minor and Major, and Jazz Melodic Minor. These are simply suggestions for variety's sake, which you can then apply to other exercises in the book.

I have also broken down the Shapes below, which will aid in your ability to transpose these by ear, and really understand what you are playing. I suggest singing the exercises while playing the suggested chord progressions on the piano, then playing over an accompaniment to really get a feel for the shapes. You could also play them over a drone, as all but the eighth shape are diatonic to the key of that chapter. You may also choose to stick to reading the written material, working things out technically and marking up any fingerings or breathing as necessary. There is something here for the classical and the jazz musician (or any kind of musician really!)

Below I have listed the sources for these shapes, along with a brief analysis of their construction. The harmonic implications are my own, not necessarily how Bach used the shapes in context.

Sources and Analysis

1. Harpsichord Concerto in f minor BWV 1056

A simple scale shape, skipping the second degree and moving up and down diatonically. The relative minor is also presented.

2. Harpsichord Concerto in f minor BWV 1056

A pair of nice ideas from the same concerto, combining 7-6 and 4-3 suspensions moving up and down.

3. Composed by the author

A chromatic neighbor tone pattern that encircles the root of the ii chord, then the third of the relative V chord, descending in a circle of fifths/fourths pattern, diatonically.

4. Composed by the author

Another neighbor tone line, this time approaching the third from below by a half step. Notice that some are diatonic, some have accidentals, but there is always a half step distance to the subsequent third. The descending line could imply this circle of fifths/fourths pattern, approaching the third of each chord.

5. Flute Sonata in G Major BWV 1039

A pair of seventh chord arpeggio shapes.

6. Toccata and Fugue in d minor BWV 565

The ascending pattern is an embellished first inversion triad, starting on the third, jumping up to the root then descending to connect to the third of the next chord. The descending pattern is another circle of fifths sequence connecting the thirds of each chord.

7. Toccata and Fugue in d minor BWV 565

Another circle of fifths sequence shape, which, like the others in this section, could be adapted to the chord progressions in the Circle of Fifths chapter by adding the relevant accidentals. Sevenths connecting to thirds, with a nice pedal point on the fifth, which becomes a brief 2-1 suspension over each following chord.

8. Cello Suite 2 Prelude in d minor BWV 1008

The only non-diatonically moving shape in this section, the first phrase,

is connecting the thirds of a circle of fifths progression, but I have harmonized it differently each time to create a satisfying chord progression. Play this with accompaniment to hear how it all works.

The descending shape outlines diminished harmony while following a descending overall line of F# E D# C# B - E:

9. Flute Partita in a minor BWV 1013

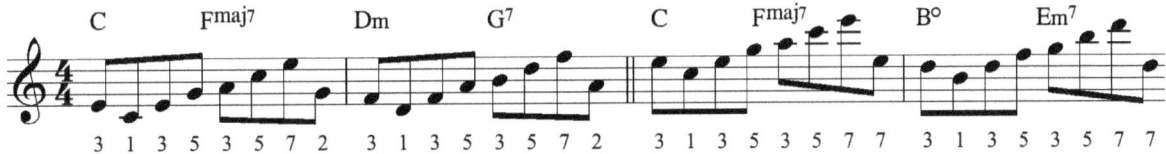

Another sequential shape connecting thirds around a series of chords in ascending fourths. Adjusting the descending sixth at the end to an octave allows the pattern to descend.

10. Cello Suite 4 in Eb Major BWV 1010

Another lovely pedal point line around the circle of fifths connecting sevenths to thirds.

11. Invention 15 in b minor BWV 786

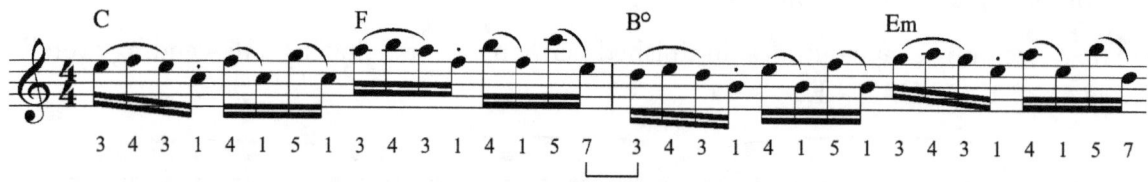

One final circle of fifths type phrase, with a 3-4-3 neighbor tone motion and a pedal point to the root as it goes around the circle, the seventh connects to the third at the end of every measure and keeps the pattern moving.

C Major

*various articulations are marked throughout this section, feel free to apply different markings or play all legato.

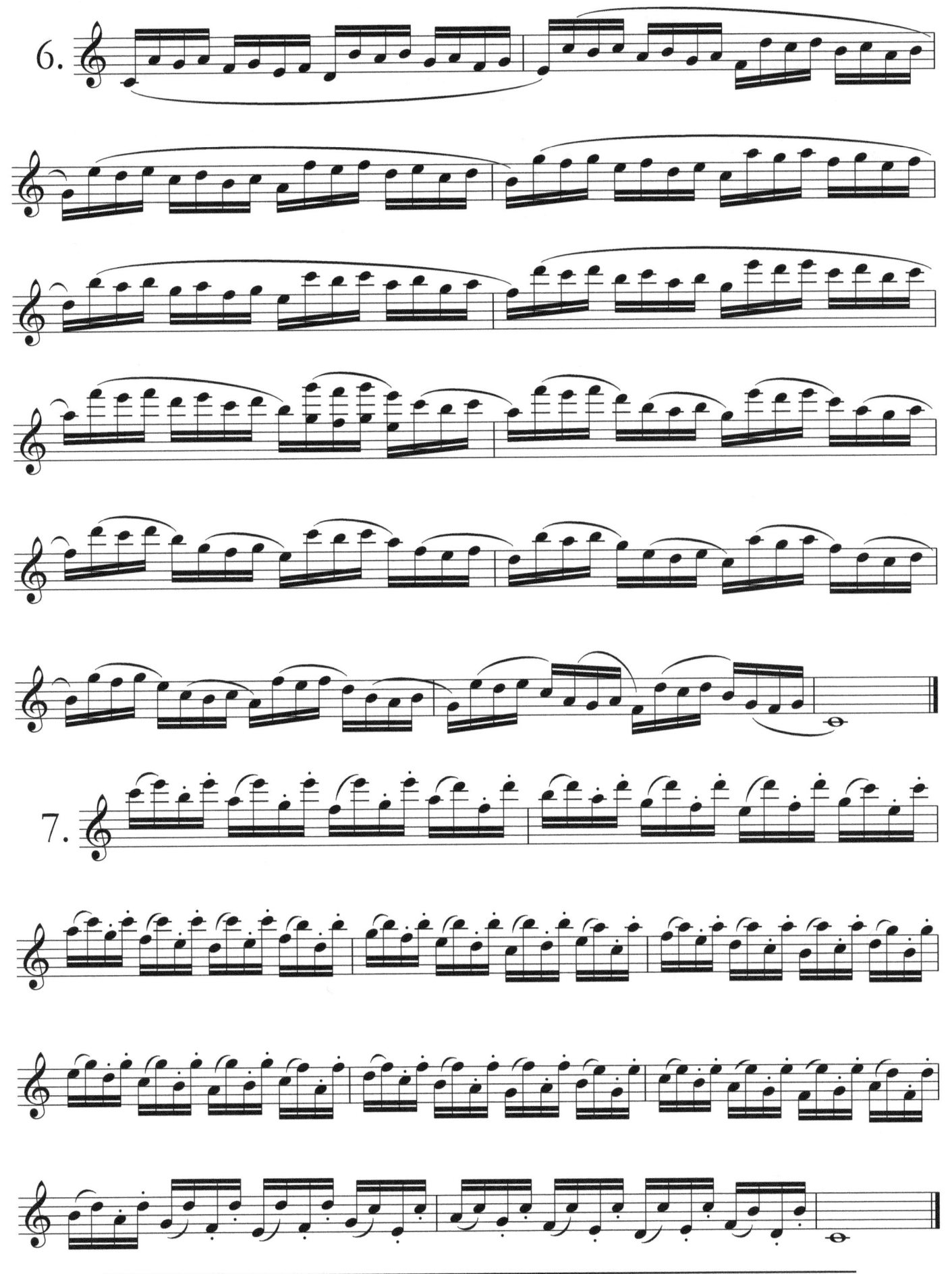

BACH SHAPES II

11.

F Major

BACH SHAPES II

BACH SHAPES II

Bb Major

Bb Harmonic Major

BACH SHAPES II

BACH SHAPES II 19

Eb Major

Eb Harmonic Minor

BACH SHAPES II

BACH SHAPES II 23

Ab Major

Db Major

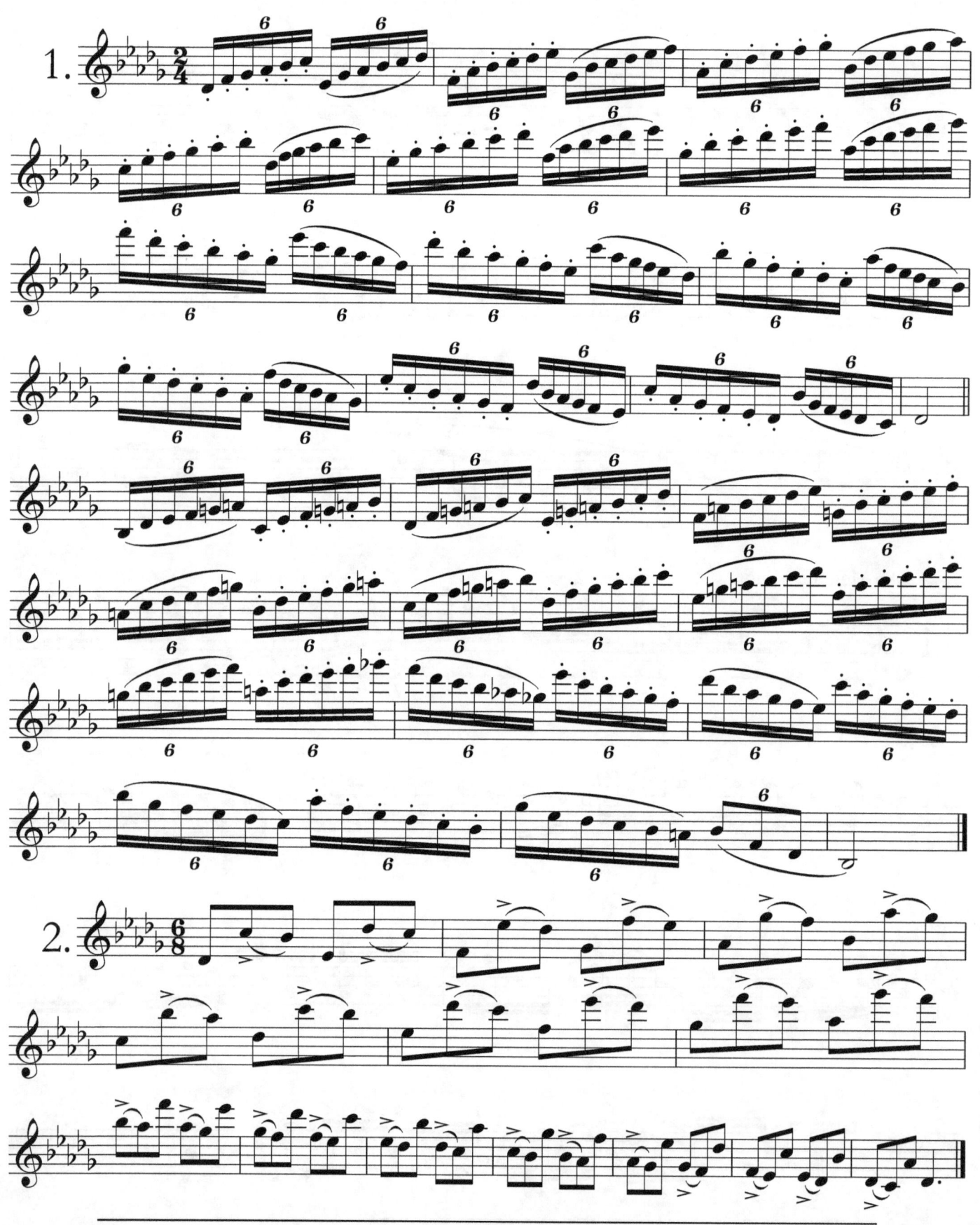

BACH SHAPES II 29

30 BACH SHAPES II

F# Major

F# Harmonic Minor

BACH SHAPES II

34 BACH SHAPES II

B Major

BACH SHAPES II 37

E Major

A Major

BACH SHAPES II 47

D Major

50 BACH SHAPES II

D Harmonic Minor

G Major

BACH SHAPES II

BACH SHAPES II 55

MINOR AND DIMINISHED SHAPES

In this section we will take a look at minor and diminished shapes. In Bach's famous *Toccata and Fugue* there are numerous examples of both, so we'll start there. But first, try this diminished warmup adapted from Artie Shaw's Clarinet Method.

Start this exercise slowly, or the 16th's will be problematic. Advanced players can carry this on into the altissimo register.

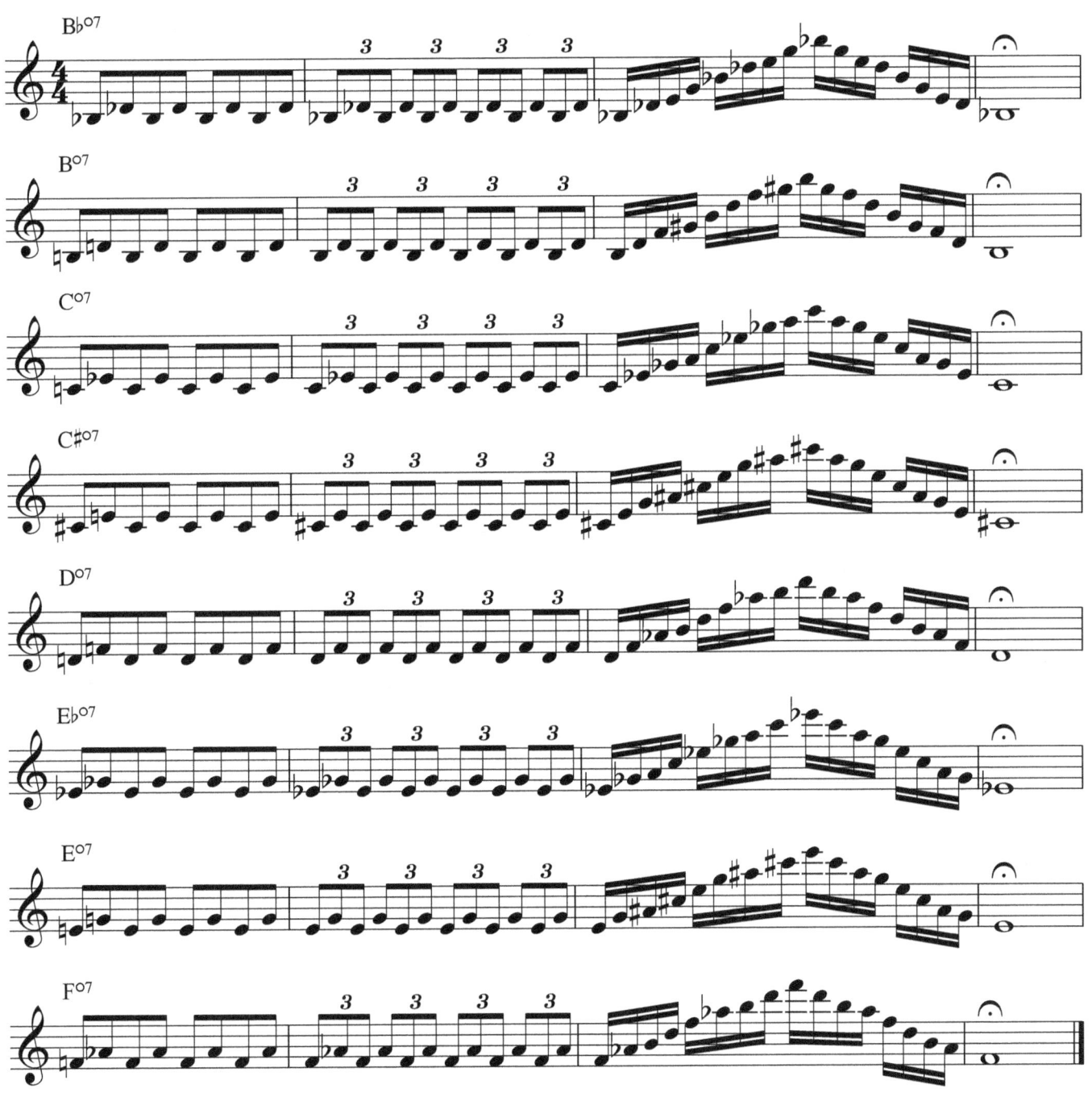

Here is one great way, from the *Toccata and Fugue,* to work on your diminished chords. I advise looping each section until it is comfortable, then moving up as shown here:

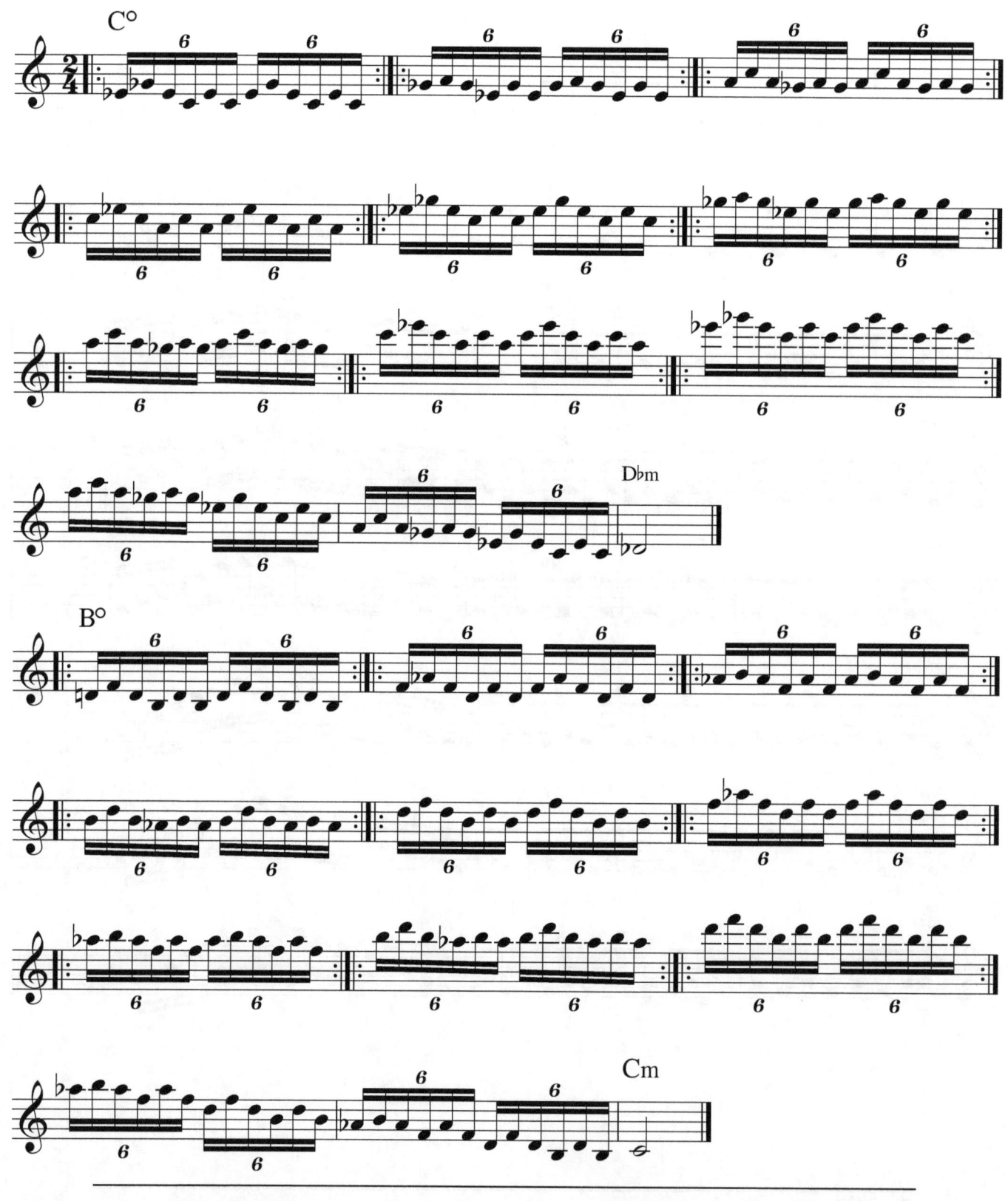

Also from the *Toccata*, a simple minor looping pattern. I call these pedal point lines, where you keep returning to a repeated note, like an open string on a violin. This is invaluable for maintaining embouchure, focusing on stillness and "inclusive" intervals, meaning a position that allows for the production of both notes, with minimal movement.

For a great increase in difficulty, try displacing the pedal note by an octave:

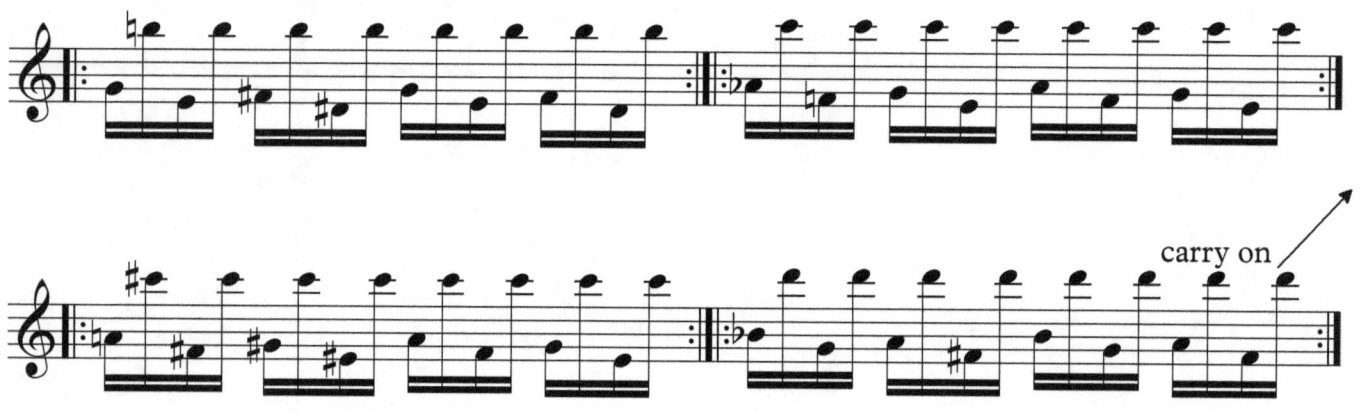

Here is a longer pedal point line from the *Fugue* section, fully realized in all 12 keys chromatically. Again, you may try displacing the pedal note up an octave for increased difficulty, or carry the exercise on into the upper register and altissimo.

Not from the *Toccata*, but a lovely diminished and minor phrase from Bach's 13th Invention in d minor, adapted to move through all 12 keys. I've analyzed the harmonic motion with dominant b9 chords, more relevant to jazz improvisers.

Here is an idea I adapted from Cannonball Adderley, alternating Major 6 chords and triads with the vii diminished, a la Barry Harris. This exercise should be played all legato, and can be played straight or swing.

To really have fun with this one, try it as a 16-bar swing tune. Improvise through the bridge.

Diminished Delight

Baroque Bebop

Here is a similar idea, now in D minor, this time not from Bach, but from Charlie Parker on the tune "Bebop." Alternating i minor and vii diminished every two beats. Keep in mind that the Edim and C#dim here are really the same chord, with different roots, and they both relate to the V7 chord. It's tension and release every two beats.

Another amazing source of ideas is the a minor Flute Partita, Bach's greatest piece for solo woodwind. We've already used one idea in Shape #9 from the first section, and we will see more in the coming chapters. For now, here is one tricky shape, again alternating between i and V7 and moved around the circle of fifths.

BACH SHAPES II

72 BACH SHAPES II

It is a rediscovery of the world of which I have the joy of being a part.

It fills me with awareness of the wonder of life, with a feeling of the incredible marvel of being a human being.

The music is never the same for me, never. Each day it is something new, fantastic and unbelievable.

That is **BACH**, like nature, a miracle!

—PABLO CASALS

BOOK TWO

CIRCLE OF FIFTHS HARMONIC SEQUENCES

In this section, we will look at Bach's use of the circle of fifths chord progression. A common device in baroque music, it is relevant to jazz improvisers as the basis to so many standard tunes. The sources for the six sequences on the following pages are as follows:

1. a minor Flute Partita BWV 1013
2. Kroepsch Book II for Clarinet
3. a minor Violin Concerto - Allegro BWV 1041
4. a minor Violin Concerto - Allegro BWV 1041
5. a minor Violin Concerto - Allegro Assai BWV 1041
6. d minor Violin Concerto last mvmt. BWV 1052

As each page is the same chord progression in one key it can be treated as a theme and variations. The final variation should be your own. Use the written material as a springboard to improvise on the progression. I have included numbers on the first page to indicate each notes' relationship to the chord.

The opening sequences, which are similar to the "Fly Me To The Moon" progression, are followed by an etude on the harmony to Jerome Kern's "All The Thing You Are" as well as Joseph Kosma's "Autumn Leaves," two more tunes that make use of this circle of fifths root motion.

After that there is a small section on the circle using only dominant chords, including an etude that is very useful for navigating this progression. You can extract many ideas from this etude, so spend time with each line and analyze what is happening. Playing all of these with chordal accompaniment would be beneficial, singing and playing over the roots or full harmonies.

Sequences in e minor

Sequences in a minor

Sequences in d minor

Sequences in g minor

Sequences in c minor

Sequences in f minor

Sequences in bb minor

Sequences in eb minor

Sequences in g# minor

Sequences in c# minor

Sequences in f# minor

Sequences in b minor

Feel the Kern

Samba
♩=120-160

Jon De Lucia

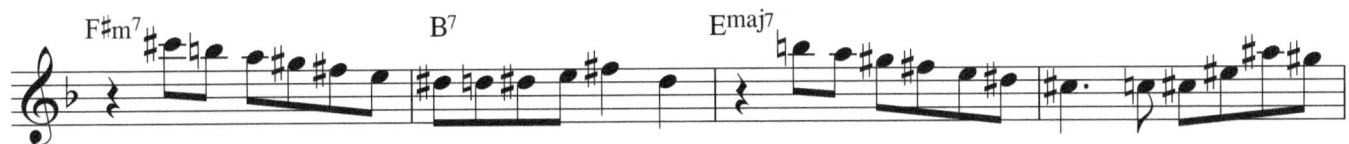

© Jon De Lucia Music

Study **BACH.**

There you will find everything.

—JOHANNES BRAHMS

Now there is music from which
a man can learn something.

—W.A. MOZART

CIRCLE OF FIFTHS PROGRESSION WITH DOMINANT CHORDS

Following the circle of fifths with only dominant chords is also a common baroque technique. Here are a few ideas from Bach's music. Notice how all of them connect from the 7th to the 3rd of the following chord, as we often do in jazz improvisation.

1. Brandenburg Concerto V

2. a minor Flute Partita

3. Harpsichord Concerto in f minor

Exploration in Fifths

Here is an exercise of my own going through a few complete cycles of the dominant progression. You will find use of chromatic approach, bebop scales, augmented chords, diminished chords, and more.

BACH AND PAUL DESMOND

One of the sources of inspiration for me to put Bach Shapes together in the first place was the great alto saxophonist Paul Desmond. He frequently makes use of baroque type patterns, especially in his early improvisations with the Dave Brubeck Quartet.

Desmond is a great place to start if you are looking for ways to apply the material from these books to standard chord progressions.

Check out Paul's solo on "Gone with the Wind" from 1954's Dave Brubeck Quartet Live at Storyville. There are at least three motivic phrases here, and it seems like in this early period Desmond was working out this kind of material more clearly than in later examples where he would break up the structure a little more. Hearing these clear early instances is a key to understanding his phrasing in later years.

Note the clever twisting of the phrase leading into the Em7 and on, adapting to the changing harmony.

Then there are a couple of measures away from the pattern before he launches into the next one at the top of the second half of the form, where this same harmonic sequence happens again:

This time he breaks away from the opening intervallic sequence pretty quickly but it informs the answering phrase in the third and fourth measures.

Finally there is this sequence over the minor harmony of the tune:

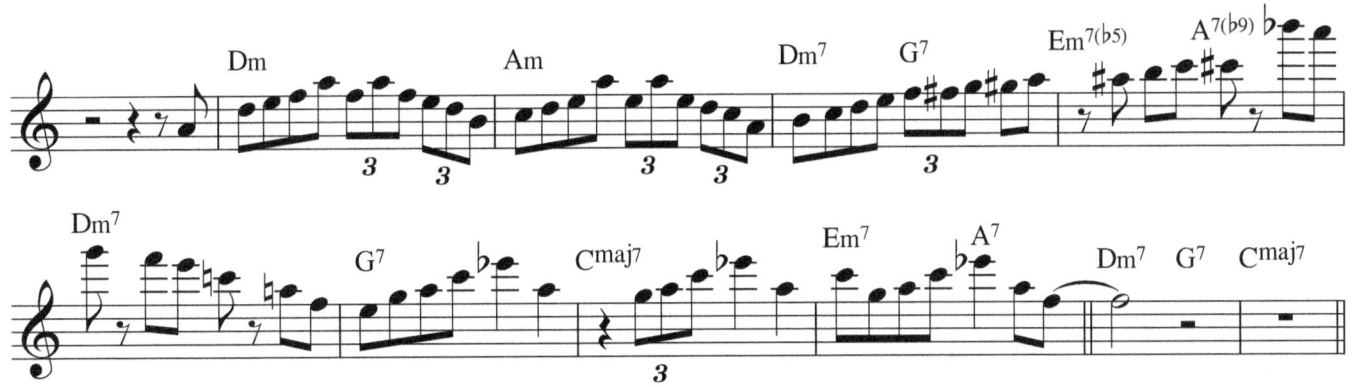

Here he carries on the rhythmic motif in the third measure but not the intervallic structure, then builds to a great peak high Bb at what is the climax of the solo and the structure of the tune, before ending with a simple blues phrase to hand off the solo to Brubeck.

Another great example is from 1954's "Stardust":

If you were to simplify this pattern, you would get the example below. The trick is in how Paul manipulates this to follow the harmony of the tune in interesting ways.

Paul has taken this basic structure, and adapted it to a C7#11, lydian dominant type sound in the second and third measures, but note how he keeps the F natural to E resolution on the 3rd beat of the second measure, as it is simply better melodicism than using the F# there. He then returns to the #11 sound until the F7, where he returns to the tonic scale, before slipping down to an Ab in the last measure, catching the flatted fifth of the Dm7b5, and then a strong C harmonic minor scale to resolve beautifully on the first beat of the next section. The solo continues after this early theme, with Desmond constantly reworking small fragments in creative ways.

These are the types of patterns found in *Bach Shapes*, so I'd like to reverse engineer an example from one of the shapes in the book. Let's take Shape Number 5 from the first *Bach Shapes*, which I took from the Second Violin Partita:

And let's apply it to Tadd Dameron's tune "Lady Bird" in the etude on the next page:

A Tadd Baroque

Bright Swing Jon De Lucia

© Jon De Lucia Music

Paul's solo on "Wintersong," which is based on the changes to "These Foolish Things," contains everything you need to know about applying Bach style arpeggiation and lines to a standard progression. Here is the whole thing:

Wintersong—Paul Desmond Solo
(changes to "These Foolish Things")

Transcribed by Jon De Lucia

BACH LOOPS

Looping melodic phrases like these can be found in many 19th century woodwind method books (Kroepsch, Klosé, Baermann).

The benefits to practicing them are clear: repetition makes progress. Repetition forces you to wrestle with one phrase at a time, learning to relax, smooth out your technique and let go of tension. Here are some ideas for practicing these:

- Play one phrase 5-10 times, relaxing your hands each time, seeing how relaxed you can get and still play.
- Try different articulations. I have left the articulations up to you here.
- Focus on your pitch, especially on wider intervals.
- Analyze the harmonic material hidden in the lines to apply it to your own improvising.
- Try playing some notes with harmonic fingerings or other alternate fingerings. Mix and match with the regular fingerings.
- Try "outlining," playing just the downbeats then gradually filling in the other notes. For more on this visit my Youtube Channel.
- Play the phrases in different octaves and different keys/modes.

Bach Loops

108   BACH SHAPES II

BACH SHAPES II 109

110 BACH SHAPES II

In **BACH,** the vital cells of music are united as the world is in God.

—GUSTAV MAHLER

ARPEGGIATION

In this section, we will look at how Bach approaches arpeggiation. This is relevant to us as improvisers, as it provides great insight into voice leading, and some nice different approaches to learning the harmony of tune. A famous example would be Prelude 1 in C Major from the Well Tempered Clavier. It is just a series of arpeggiated chords, but there is somehow a feeling of beautiful melodic continuity and drama. This is evident in our first example, taken from Cello Suite No. 4, the Prelude in Eb Major. I have reproduced the first two pages here.

Cello Suite No. 4: Prelude

Penciling in chord symbols is a great way to see how the notes relate harmonically.

Another great example comes from the a minor Flute Partita, here:

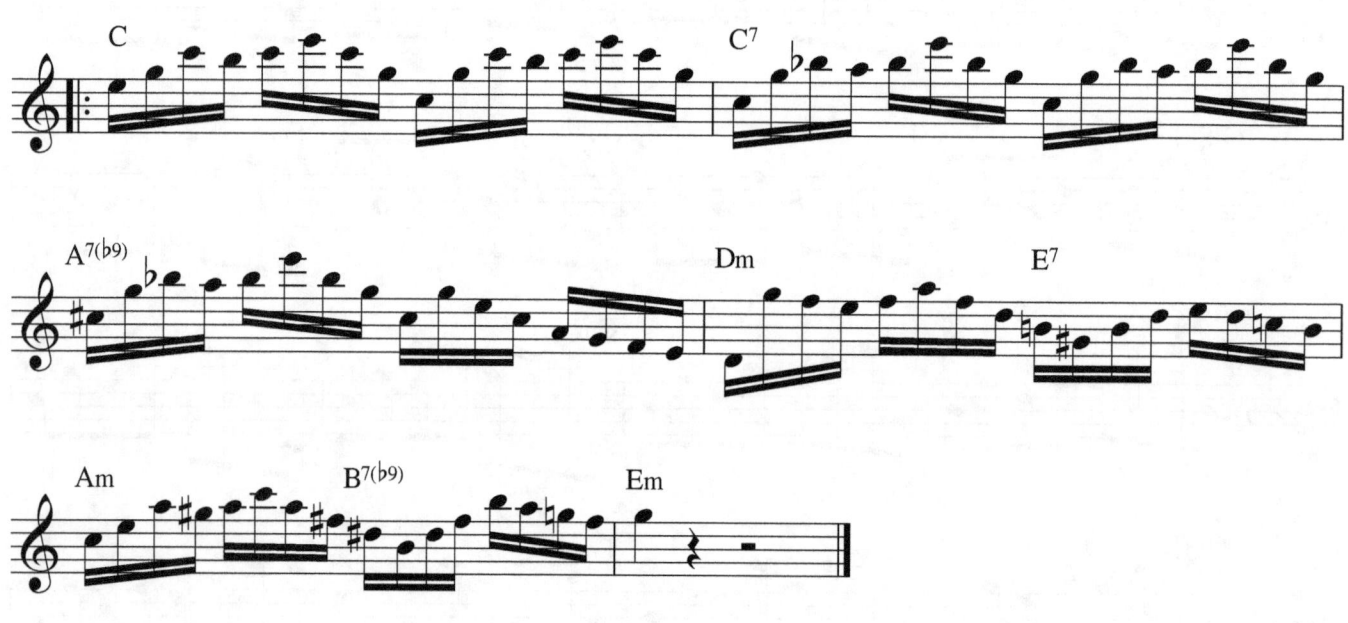

116 BACH SHAPES II

Now let's take that basic shape and try and put it through a standard set of changes, in this case, Ray Noble's "Cherokee." If you want to play this study with a jazz backing track, play the 16ths as 8ths.

Cheroque

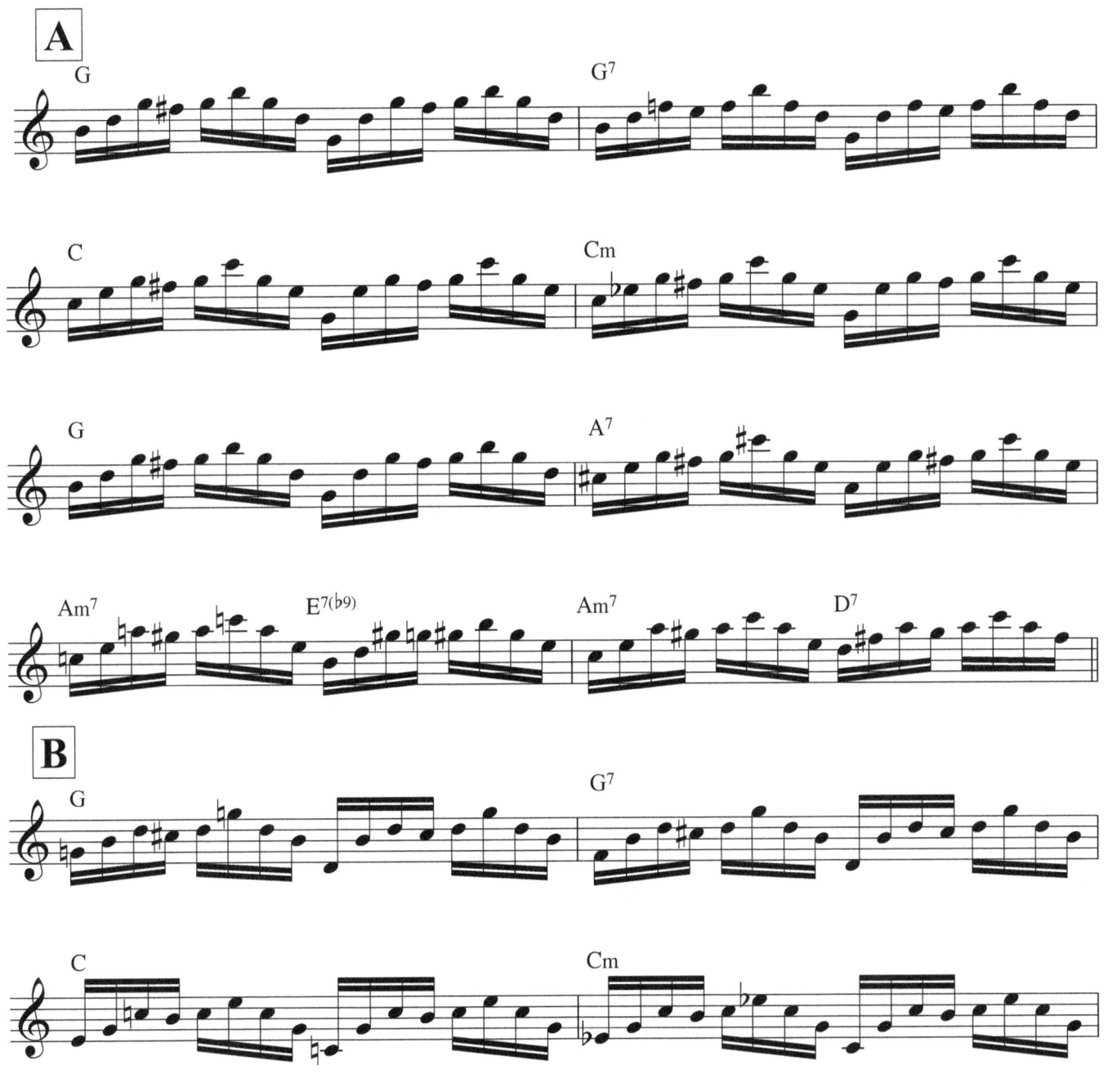

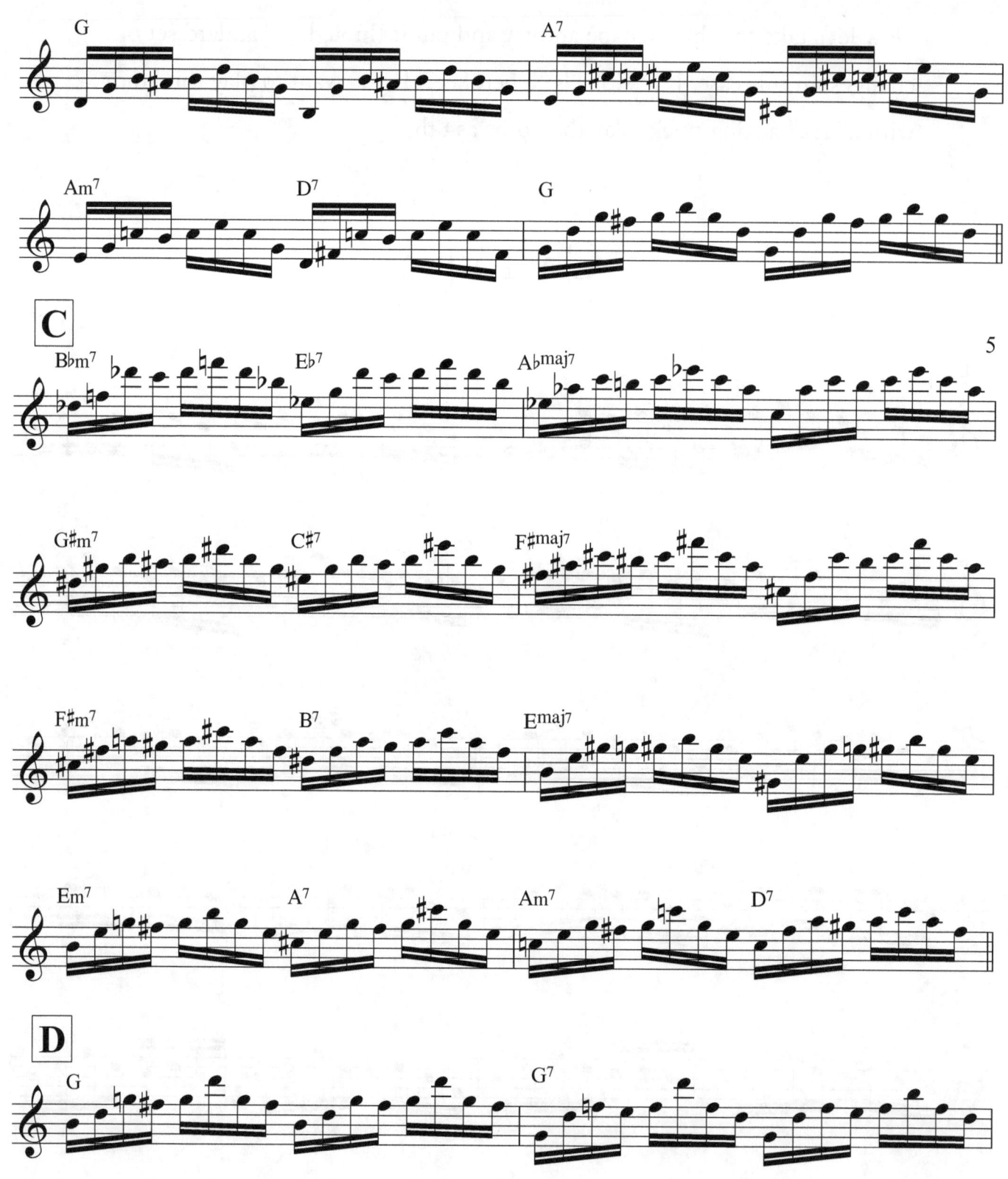

Notice that the inversion I start with for each section will determine the voice leading, resulting in slightly different sequences each time. The key is to do this on the fly, hearing the connections and taking your time to figure out the best way to navigate the changes. In fact, you may want to start just by connecting triads through a tune.

For example, here is "All of Me" in root position triads, key of A Major for alto sax, just the first 16 bars.

Then here is same section, with voice leading. This means I'm finding the closest inversion to the chord I am currently on, with as many common tones and as little large movement as possible. The results are more musical. I can't stress enough how much singing and playing this exercise improved my ears and ability to hear harmony.

The next step is to take a Bach-type pattern through the tune, incorporating voice leading. Make sure to play this lightly, and focusing on time with a metronome. Make music out of it!

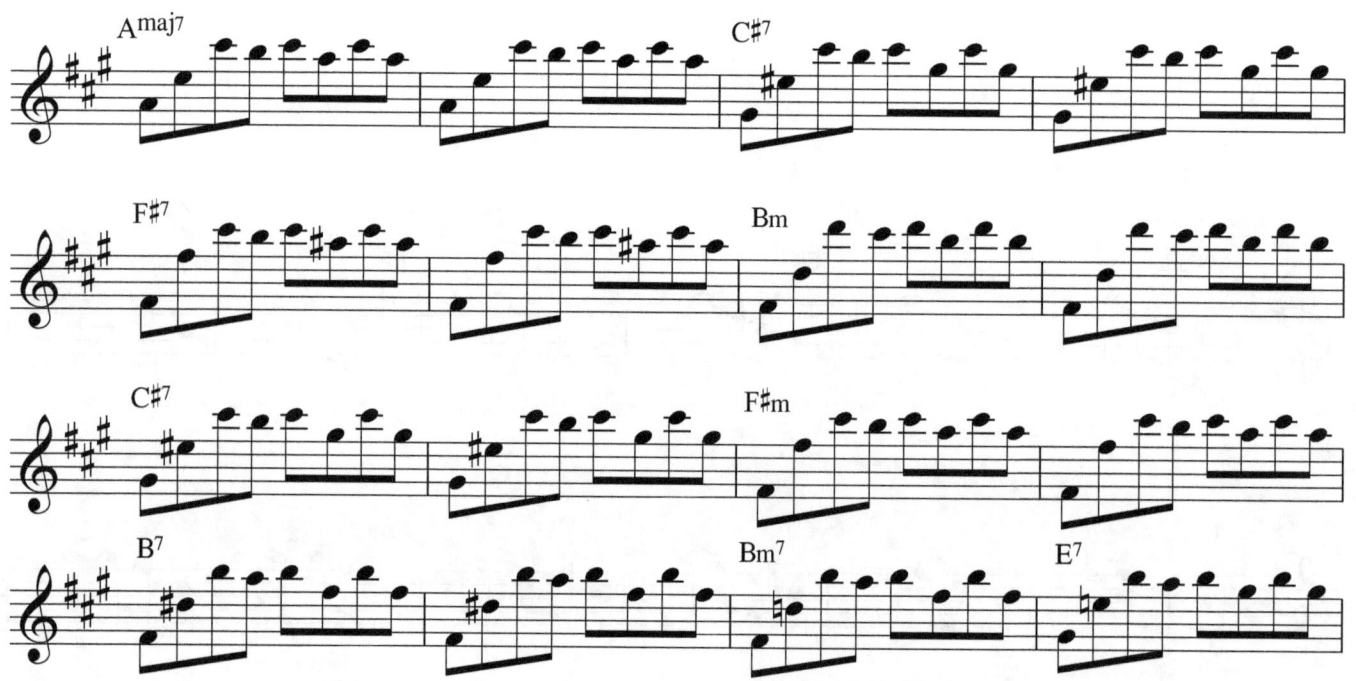

Now try your own. Below I have given five different shapes from Bach's music that I would encourage you to try and take through a tune of your choice.

ADDITIONAL ETUDES

This section includes four more etudes. Three are based on standard progressions, while one is more spontaneous and meant to be played freely in a legato style. Use the audio tracks to learn how to interpret these melodies.

You will recognize many of the shapes used from earlier in this book, and some from the previous book. Enjoy and remember to make music!

Going Bach Home

Jon De Lucia

Musaeum Clausum

Jon De Lucia

Freely

Jesu, Jes' Me

Jon De Lucia

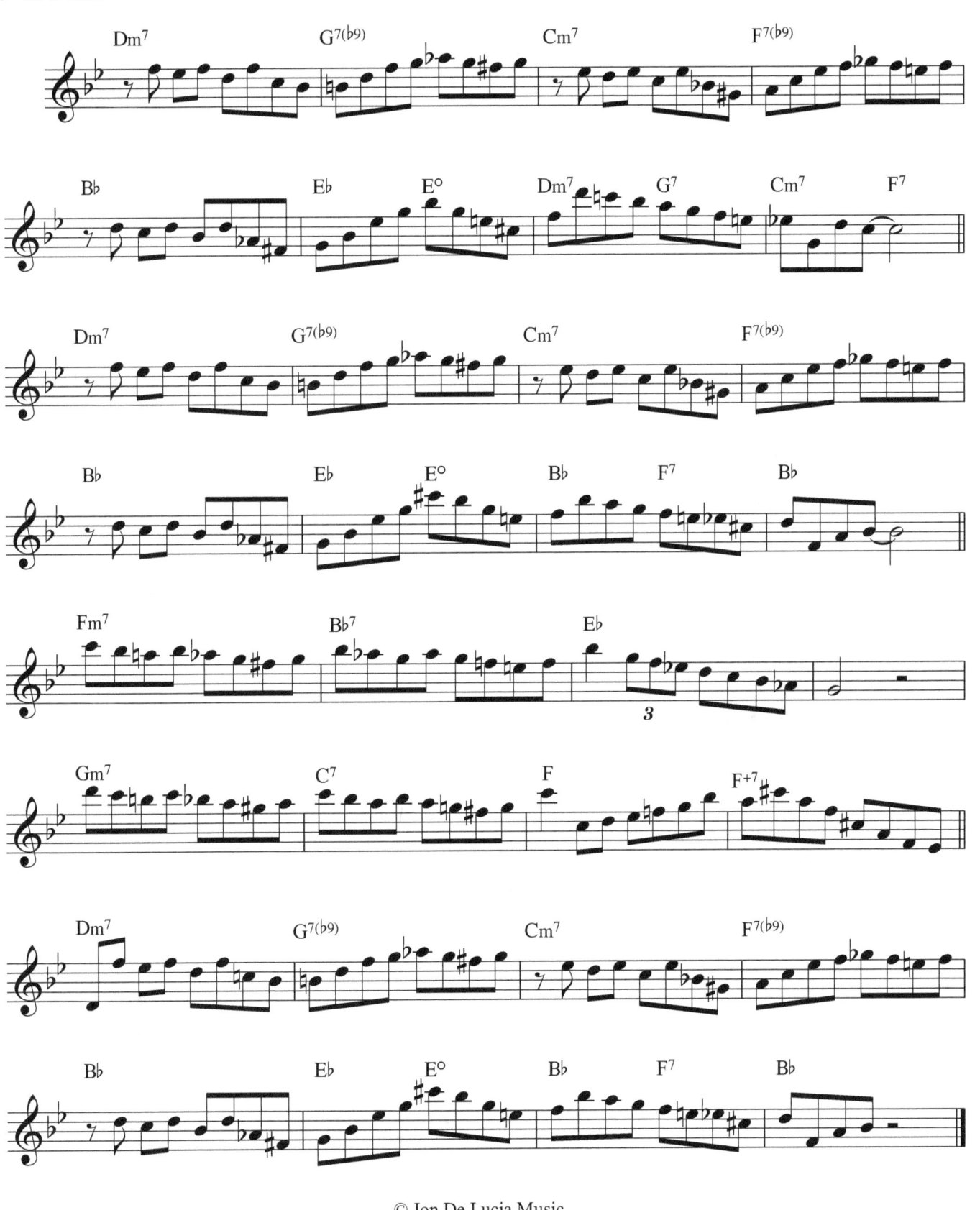

Love Me Or Liebe Me

Funky Swing
♩=90

Jon De Lucia

ABOUT THE AUTHOR

Jon De Lucia is a jazz saxophonist and clarinetist based in Brooklyn, NY. He holds an MA in Jazz Studies from the City College of New York and has studied with Lee Konitz, Andrew Sterman, Bill Pierce, George Garzone, Greg Osby, Joe Lovano and many more. His interest in the music of the baroque led to the forming of the Luce Trio, a new take on early music for saxophone, electric guitar and bass. Between this group and his work as leader/arranger of the Jon De Lucia Octet he has fused the counterpoint of J.S. Bach with a West Coast jazz sensibility. He can be found regularly performing in the NYC area. *Author photo © Matt Harvey*

www.ingramcontent.com/pod-product-compliance
Lightning Source LLC
Chambersburg PA
CBHW081415080526
44589CB00016B/2541